IMAGES
of America

THE GREAT BOSTON FIRE
OF 1872

Three businessmen stand on broken pieces of granite that were once a part of buildings on Pearl Street. The walls of granite imploded as the intensity of the fire increased, leaving grotesquely shaped ruins of the once fashionable business blocks that had been built in downtown Boston.

IMAGES
of America

THE GREAT BOSTON FIRE
OF 1872

Anthony Mitchell Sammarco

ARCADIA

First published 1997
Copyright © Anthony Mitchell Sammarco, 1997

ISBN 0-7524-0559-4

Published by Arcadia Publishing,
an imprint of the Chalford Publishing Corporation,
One Washington Center, Dover, New Hampshire 03820.
Printed in Great Britain

Library of Congress Cataloging-in-Publication Data applied for

Businessmen stand in front of the ruins of what was once the store of Clark Plympton & Company on Summer Street the day after the fire was stopped.

Contents

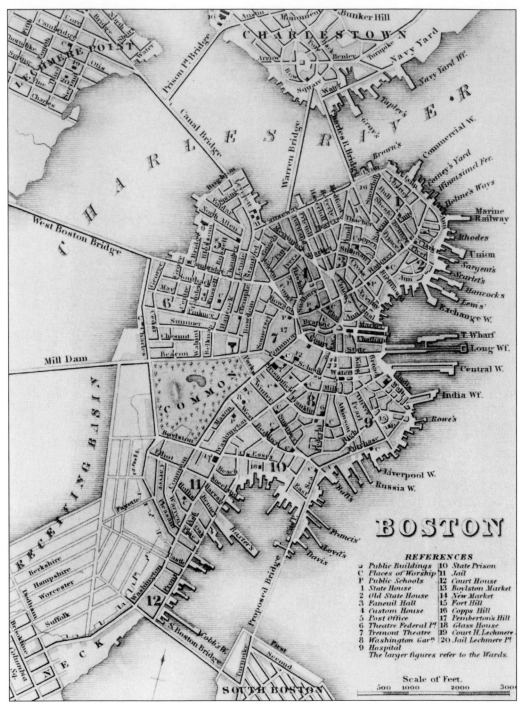

BOSTON

Boston was incorporated as a city on March 4, 1822, and was to undergo tremendous changes during the next five decades. By the time this 1833 map was drawn, the South End (lower right) had been infilled on either side of Washington Street. The Public Garden, between Beacon and Boylston Streets, would be completed in 1837. Downtown Boston was already experiencing an increase in commercial development, with a displacement of the residential quarter.

Introduction

The Great Boston Fire of 1872 destroyed much of downtown Boston, an area of 40 acres bound by Summer, Washington, and Milk Streets and the waterfront. The fire destroyed not only 775 buildings and millions of dollars of merchandise, but also swept away old Boston, enabling architects to rebuild the city as its nickname, the "Hub of the Universe," gave credence.

Boston was incorporated as a city on March 4, 1822, and in the next five decades (1822–1872,) underwent many changes. From a town primarily inhabited by the descendants of the Puritans who had settled the Shawmut Peninsula in 1630, Boston had become known in the nineteenth century as the "Athens of America," in regards to its liberal aspects of religion, education, and philosophical thought as something to be emulated by other cities in the young Republic. As a major port on the East Coast, Boston was the landing site of numerous European immigrants who sought a better life, and new arrivals from Ireland, Germany, and the British Isles began to swell the population; so much so that by the time of the Civil War, one half of Boston's residents were foreign born.

In the 1830s, because of the increased population, the city government sought ways to augment land usage, and the result was the beginning of the infilling of land. As early as the turn of the nineteenth century, the top of Beacon Hill had been cut down and used to create the flat of Beacon Hill. By 1816, a toll road was laid out connecting Boston to Brookline and was known as the Milldam, the present Beacon Street. However, as Boston changed, the downtown area of the city continued to remain a charming enclave with well-designed houses. Known as the South End of Boston (in contrast to the North End), the area of Summer, Arch, Franklin, Federal, and Pearl Streets had fashionable townhouses set on tree-shaded streets and surrounding parks. By the 1790s, Charles Bulfinch, a "gentleman architect," began to change the architectural mask of Boston with the introduction of connected townhouses, following his tour of Europe. The first townhouses sharing a uniform facade in Boston was the Tontine Crescent, a row of sixteen brick townhouses sharing a facade that was punctuated by a pedimented pavilion in the center. Bulfinch had the brick townhouses painted grey to emulate the more expensive stone, and the development proved an architectural success, though a financial debacle for him. By the turn of the nineteenth century, Bulfinch had turned to architecture as his profession, and he designed numerous neo-classical townhouses for the gentry of Federal Boston.

By 1822, when the voters of Boston incorporated the City of Boston, changes were taking place, such as the reuse of the Old State House as the first Boston City Hall and the building of Quincy Market just east of Fanueil Hall. Designed by Alexander Parris between 1824 and 1826, Quincy Market was named after the second mayor of Boston, Josiah Quincy. The downtown district, once residential, had begun to attract commercial concerns, especially along the waterfront. By the 1850s, the once exclusive residential enclaves of Franklin and Summer Streets had been invaded by commerce, and in 1858, Bulfinch's Tontine Crescent was swept away for stores and warehouses of granite that were designed by Gridley J. Fox Bryant. Ironically, Bryant maintained the gently sweeping curve of Franklin Street in the facades of his new buildings, thereby perpetuating one of Bulfinch's original streetscapes. By the Civil War, Boston's population had swelled to 165,000, and the area was almost wholly deserted by the well-to-do families for Beacon Hill, the Back Bay, and the new South End.

Though the area of Summer Street was rebuilt in the 1860s as a commercial district, with four- and five-story buildings of granite and stone, the zoning issue was never addressed, and the water supply, which was sufficient for residences, proved wholly inadequate for commercial concerns. The narrow streets, many of which were lined with majestic shade trees, proved too narrow for traffic and were inadequate for a bustling shopping district. By 1872, the downtown area of Boston was almost entirely commercial and was a cause for concern by the city's fire department. The conditions, never corrected though constantly reported, seemed to reinforce the concept of inadequate service in the advent of a fire, as the fire department consisted of "106 permanent and 363 call men, 21 steam fire engines, 7 ladder trucks, 11 independent hose companies and 3 wagons carrying chemical hand extinguishers." The city, though being built with impressive buildings, was unprepared for a potential fire, and John S. Damrell, Boston's fire chief, warned of the possibility of a calamity, especially after the disastrous fire in Chicago in 1871.

The story of the Great Boston Fire of November 9 and 10, 1872, has been recounted many times and in diverse ways, but none were more eloquent than in a sermon by Reverend Dr. Webb of the Shawmut Church of Boston. His view of the fire was straightforward and said that "We are under a government which embraces the minutest events. Some natural law is violated and the penalty follows. Combustible roofs, like the grass of the prairie, fed the fire as it flew. Has it not been burned into our souls that only men wise in foresight, quick to discern, prompt to act, capable of leading in the hour of danger, should be intrusted with the city's affairs? The penalty for imperfect work or design, as in a ship of a safe, is disaster. This calamity is the work of Providence; but he who lets matters rest there without investigation is a fool." This view was echoed by Reverend Henry Ward Beecher of New York, and there was not a church in Boston whose pastor did not make some reference to the fire and its implications in the weeks following the fire.

Through the efforts of a swarm of photographers who ventured into the area of the burnt district and perched their cameras on stone-heaps in the most picturesque quarters, we have a series of images that chronicle this great disaster. The Great Boston Fire of 1872 destroyed not just 40 acres of the city, but created a new basis point whereby Boston could be rebuilt to reflect its past achievements and extol the virtues of its accomplishments. In this photographic history, the development of Boston and the rebuilding of the city following the fire create an exciting book that addresses the story in a startling and visual manner.

By Heaven! it is a splendid sight to see,
For one who hath no friend, no brother, there.

One

Old Summer Street

Summer Street, in a print from the 1820s, offers the quintessential reason why it was such a charming enclave in the early nineteenth century—New South Society. This octagonal granite church designed by Charles Bulfinch and built in 1814 at "Church Green," the junction of Bedford and Summer Streets, is located at the center of the picture. The neighborhood was to remain residential until the late 1850s, when it eventually gave way to commercial concerns.

The Vassall-Gardner Mansion was built about 1727 on Summer Street, the present site of Macy's (the former Jordan Marsh Department Store). An impressive mid-eighteenth-century house, it was demolished in 1854 by George Gardner, who was to build the block where C.F. Hovey's Store was located.

Charles Bulfinch (1763–1848) was a gentleman architect whose sense of perspective and architectural understanding enabled him to create a new Boston between 1790 and 1815. Following his graduation from Harvard College in 1781, he took the grand tour of Europe and enlightened himself to the urbane architecture of the neo-classical period, which he in turn introduced to Boston.

The Tontine Crescent on Franklin Place (now Street) was a study in elegance and proportion. Designed by Bulfinch and completed in 1795, it was a row of sixteen connected townhouses with a central pavilion, and was financed by tontine, whereby the capital stock was divided equally among the initial investors after a specific period of time. The second floor of the central pavilion was the location of the Boston Library Society, a private library that has since merged with the Boston Athenaeum, and the third floor was the first headquarters of the Massachusetts Historical Society. The arch below led through to Summer Street and is perpetuated by Arch Street.

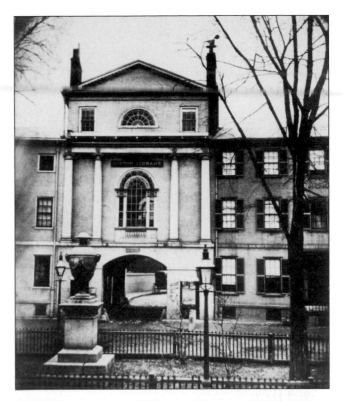

The north side of Franklin Place had four duplex townhouses similar in design to the Tontine Crescent. Freestanding, they too were built of brick and painted stone grey with white trim to resemble the connected townhouses across the square.

Franklin Place was laid out by Bulfinch as a gently sweeping curve that created a concave facade facing a central tree-shaded park. Bulfinch was undoubtedly emulating the parks of London when he laid out the street, and the neighborhood remained an attractive oasis from business concerns until it was swept away in 1858 for commercial warehouses.

An 1835 print of Franklin Place, looking southeast from Washington Street, shows the duplex houses Bulfinch had designed on the left and the sweeping Tontine Crescent on the right. The spire of the Federal Street Church, designed by Bulfinch in 1809, rises just beyond the park.

The north side of Franklin Place had four duplex houses designed by Bulfinch. Photographed in 1855, they faced the park that had been embellished by not just shade trees, but a large stone urn that Bulfinch brought back from Europe and placed in the center of Franklin Place in memory of Benjamin Franklin. The urn was later placed on Bulfinch's grave at Mount Auburn Cemetery after the park and houses were swept away in 1858.

The Cathedral of the Holy Cross was designed by Charles Bulfinch for the first Catholic bishop of Boston, Jean-Louis A.M. LeFebvre de Cheverus, at the far end of the Tontine Crescent on Franklin Place. Built in 1803, it was an impressive design that had been done gratis by the architect and whose building fund had been contributed to by prominent Bostonians. On the left is the Gothic-revival spire of the Federal Street Church designed by Bulfinch and built in 1809.

13

A print of the Cathedral of the Holy Cross in the 1840s shows how impressive the neo-classical designs by Bulfinch could be to the overall streetscape. Franklin Place was lined with elegant brick townhouses. On the east end, the Cathedral of The Holy Cross was dedicated in 1803 at the corner of Devonshire Street, serving a primarily French and Irish Catholic congregation until 1868, after which the present cathedral was begun on Washington Street in the South End.

Charles Bulfinch designed this three-story mansion at the corner of Summer and Arch Streets for the merchant John Tappan. An elegant mansion, the Tappan House was similar to the first house Bulfinch designed in 1796 for Harrison Gray Otis on Cambridge Street, now the headquarters of the Society for the Preservation of New England Antiquities (SPNEA).

The duplex mansion at the corner of Summer and Kingston Streets was once the home of such prominent Bostonians as Israel Thorndike, Governor Edward Everett, George Blake, and Dr. Nathaniel Frothingham. Four stories in height, this brick mansion was an elegant version of the townhouses then being built in London.

15

The Welles-Gray duplex mansion was built about 1812 at the corner of Summer and Kingston Streets, directly behind the New South Church, whose spire can be seen on the far left. The house was built for the Welles and Gray families.

The Boston Theatre was designed by Charles Bulfinch at the corner of Franklin and Federal Streets, just east of the Tontine Crescent. Opened in 1794, many Bostonians perceived theatrical performances as being the Devil's workshop and were not surprised when the building was destroyed by fire in 1798. Promptly rebuilt, it served as a theatre for over fifty years.

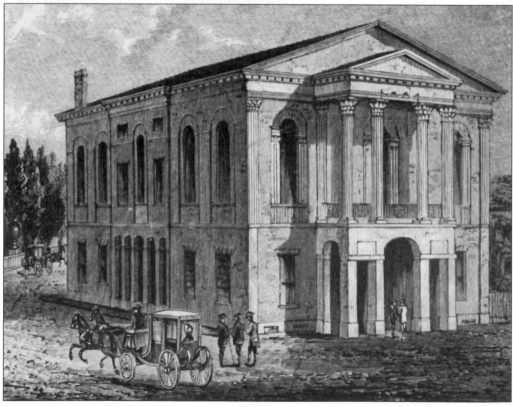

Bulfinch's development of Boston during the Federal period was to include "Colonnade Row," a row of connected townhouses built in 1810 on Tremont Street between West and Mason Streets, facing the Boston Common.

Colonnade Row, comprised of twenty-four townhouses, shared a common roofline and red brick facade and faced the Lafayette Mall on the Boston Common. A cast-iron balcony ran the length of the rowhouses along the piano nobile, or second floor. Notice the streetcar tracks along Tremont Street in the foreground.

Winthrop Place, now known as Devonshire Street, was built with small townhouses in the early nineteenth century. Looking from Summer Street, Winthrop Place was a charming tree-lined street; on the far right is the home of Rufus Choate.

On the opposite side of Winthrop Place were, from the left, the homes of George Bond, Henry Cabot, and Henry Cabot Lodge.

Daniel Webster lived in this townhouse at the bend of Summer and High Streets. Notice Summer Street on the left with the great profusion of trees and shrubbery, which offered cool shade in the heat of the summer.

Daniel Webster later sold his townhouse to Peter Chardon Brooks, one of Boston's earliest millionaires, and the Brooks family lived here until the neighborhood became commercial in nature. The house was demolished in 1862 to make way for commercial blocks.

The mansion of Judge Thomas Dawes was at 37 Purchase Street. Built *c.* 1795, it was an impressive three-story house that has been attributed to Charles Bulfinch.

The home of Captain Timothy Dalton was built in 1758 and stood at the corner of Congress and Water Streets, the present site of the McCormick Post Office Building. Congress Street was a combination of Atkinson and Dalton Streets and renamed as such in 1854.

Samuel May's home was at 234 Congress Street, at the corner of Purchase Street. The house survived the Great Boston Fire, though a portion was demolished and the remainder became commercial space until the house was entirely demolished in 1889. (Courtesy of David Rooney.)

Nathaniel Bowditch and Oliver Eldredge shared this duplex mansion on Otis Place, which ran from Summer to Franklin Streets, opposite Kingston Street.

This row of granite townhouses was occupied, from the left, by Joshua Blake, Samuel Cabot, and George Bancroft.

Looking down Otis Place from Summer Street, one can see that many of the townhouses built on the streets off Summer Street were relatively simple in comparison to the houses designed by Bulfinch on Franklin Place.

High Street, in this print of 1822, had a bucolic setting with the tree-shaded home of Jeffrey Richardson in the center and the grand mansion of Jonathan Harris, often referred to as "Harris' Folly," in the background.

Samuel Whitwell built his home on Winthrop Place, now Winthrop Square, in 1822.

Fort Hill Square was between Oliver and High Streets and was laid out on the site of the former Fort Hill, or the South Battery. The townhouses faced a park, initially known as Washington Place, which at the center of the hilltop had tree-lined paths.

Fort Hill Square had already become home to some of the immigrants settling in Boston when this photograph was taken in 1865. The once elegant townhouses had now given way to tenements with many families often sharing one room of the house, causing concern among city officials. Between 1866 and 1872, Fort Hill was leveled and the soil was used to infill Atlantic Avenue and parts of Bay Village.

The spire of the Old South Meeting House projected through the shade trees on Milk Street in this print of 1811. Laid out in 1708, Milk Street was a combination of residential and commercial buildings by the early nineteenth century, and it retained much of its early charm.

Chauncy Street, which runs from Summer to Essex Streets, was the site of the First Church in Boston (on the right) and the Chauncy Hall School, which had been founded by Gideon Thayer in 1828. The First Church had moved here in 1808 from Washington Street and eventually moved in 1867 to the corner of Berkeley and Marlborough Streets in the new Back Bay. Chauncy Hall School moved to Boylston Street, near Dartmouth Street, in 1873.

The First Church, which had been founded in 1632, was an Unitarian church designed by Asher Benjamin (1773–1845) and built in 1808 on Chauncy Place (now Street).

Chauncy Street, as seen from Exeter Place in 1860, still had well-kept townhouses with the Chauncy Hall School and the First Church in the distance.

The New South Church was built in 1814 at the junction of Bedford and Summer Streets. Designed by Charles Bulfinch as an octagonal church and built of granite, it lent its name to a small grass plot in front which was known as "Church Green." The church was an impressive addition to Summer Street, but as the area became more commercial in the early 1860s, the congregation eventually moved and the church was closed in 1868.

The pedimented porch of the New South Church was an impressive aspect of Church Green, as seen from Bedford Street. In the distance are the Summer Street homes of Henry Gassett and William Sturgis.

By the time this pencil sketch of Summer Street was done by Sarah Hodges in 1846, the street had impressive houses interspersed with churches. Trinity Church, a Gothic design by George Dexter, was completed in 1829 and was built of rough-hewn granite blocks. In the distance can be seen the spire of the Park Street Church, built in 1809 at the corner of Tremont and Park Streets by Peter Banner.

Trinity Church was flanked by Thorndike Hall on the left and Mercantile Hall on the right. As late as 1858, Summer Street continued to be the dwelling place for wealthy "old residents" of Boston.

By 1868 when Reverend Phillips Brooks was settled at Trinity Church, Summer Street was entirely commercial with only a few trees as a remembrance of its once bucolic past.

By the 1860s, Summer Street was a major route for the horse-drawn streetcars connecting Boston and South Boston via the Broadway Railway. The spire of the New South Church rises above a tree on Summer Street, pictured about 1862; on the right is the former home of Daniel Webster.

Saint Stephen's Church was built in 1844 on Purchase Street. Serving a small Episcopal congregation, the church was destroyed in the Great Boston Fire. (Courtesy of the BPL.)

The Tremont House, designed by Isaiah Rogers and built in 1829 at the corner of Tremont and Beacon Streets, was Boston's first luxury hotel. Offering a dining room, private reception rooms, private bedrooms, and flush toilets, it was not only convenient but considered the height of fashion.

The Bromfield House was a small hotel on Bromfield Street near Washington Street. Photographed in 1858, men pose in front of the hotel with the facade of the Bromfield Street Methodist Church on the far right.

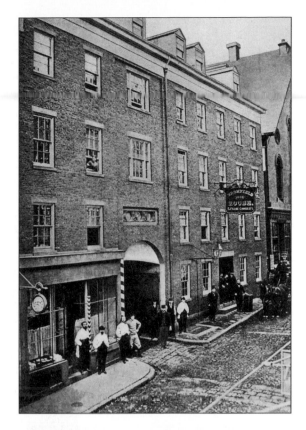

Members participating in the Methodist Episcopal Conference in 1843 at the Bromfield Street Church are depicted in this print. The interior of the church was not unlike most New England meetinghouses of the early nineteenth century. (Courtesy of William H. Pear.)

The Brazer Building was designed by Isaiah Rogers and built on State Street, between Devonshire Street and Quaker Lane. On the left is the Traveller Building at the corner of Congress Street, and on the far right is the Old State House, which became Boston City Hall in 1822. The Brazer Building was built on the site of the original First Church, built in 1632.

Washington Street, seen from Dock Square in the 1860s, shows the hodgepodge of buildings lining the streets in downtown Boston prior to the fire. The wood-framed houses had been converted to commercial concerns, and six-story buildings were interspersed with smaller structures. The area had changed from residential to commercial in nature so quickly that zoning could not be enacted.

Two

The Advent of Commercialism

Washington Street, known as Marlborough Street in the eighteenth century, had become a commercial area by the 1840s, with these granite buildings being built opposite School Street. Three stories in height with a shared roof, the buildings replaced the once fashionable residences that were fast disappearing in the downtown section of Boston. (Courtesy of the BPL.)

The Old State House, which was rebuilt after the 1711 fire, became Boston City Hall on March 4, 1822. Serving as the center of city government for the next two decades, the building became a commercial space after the city offices were moved to School Street. As seen in this 1870 photograph, the Old State House was to contain numerous businesses, all of which seemed to advertise on the exterior walls.

The Suffolk County Court House on School Street became Boston City Hall in 1841, after moving from the Old State House. Built by Charles Bulfinch in 1810, it was an impressive ashlar building with flanking wings.

A statue of Benjamin Franklin was dedicated on September 17, 1856, in front of Boston City Hall with the tolling of bells, the firing of cannon, and a procession that seemed as if it might go on forever. A throng of Bostonians came together to honor Franklin, who left a bequest to Bostonians that was later to be used to establish the Franklin Institute and purchase a tract of land that is now known as Franklin Park.

Franklin's statue, which was sculpted by Richard S. Greenough, was surrounded by a cast-iron fence and was originally in the center of the walkway to Boston City Hall.

The Merchants' Exchange was designed by Isaiah Rogers and built on State Street, just east of Congress Street. An impressive Greek Revival structure with Corinthian columns, it was built of Quincy granite. A man with a telescope looks toward Boston Harbor in anticipation of arriving ships, most of which were owned by members of the exchange. (Courtesy of the Boston Athenaeum.)

The old Boston Custom House was built on Custom House Street and was a brick structure surmounted by a gilded eagle.

The second Boston Custom House was designed by Ammi Burnham Young (1800–1874) and was completed in 1847, after twelve years of construction. A granite structure with fluted Doric columns, it originally faced the waterfront which was just to the east (on the right) of the steps; however, the area was infilled in the late nineteenth century. The present office tower was built in 1915 and was designed by the architectural firm of Peabody and Stearns.

The Merchants' Exchange was built in 1842 by Isaiah Rogers (1800–1869). By the time of the Civil War, when this photograph was taken, it was in the midst of banking and investment houses, which proliferated State Street. The impressive temple-fronted structure was later replaced by the Exchange Building.

Thorndike Hall was on Summer Street, between Washington and Hawley Streets. Here the Masonic Bodies in Boston met after their temple (in Winthrop House at the corner of Tremont and Boylston Streets) was destroyed by fire in 1866. By 1870, it was the site of George Hill & Company.

C.F. Hovey & Company were importers, jobbers, and dry goods retailers. The store was on Summer Street near Washington Street, and was built in 1863 on the site of the Vassall-Gardner Mansion, now the site of Macy's Department Store.

Looking east on Summer Street from Washington Street in 1871, this view shows the buildings (on the right) that were built on the site of the Vassall-Gardner Mansion. In the distance can be seen the spire of the New South Society, which faced Church Green at the junction of Summer and Bedford Streets.

Rice and Hutchins' Buildings were built at the corner of Summer and High Streets, on the site of Daniel Webster's home and garden. These buildings were four stories in height with a mansard roof, setting the architectural tone of the area as it continued to become more commercial after the Civil War.

Franklin Street had been rebuilt as as a commercial district after Bulfinch's Tontine Crescent was swept away between 1858 and 1859. J. Gridley Fox Bryant (1816–1899) rebuilt the area with four-story granite stores and warehouses, retaining the gently sweeping curve Bulfinch had introduced to the street when he built the Crescent.

The south side of Franklin Street had a Federal townhouse at the corner of Hawley Street with J. Gridley Fox Bryant's commercial block of 1858–59 curving toward Arch Street.

William H. Horton & Company was an importer and dealer in French silk goods; their "millinery warehouse" was at 12 and 14 Franklin Street, near Washington Street, in a building that replaced one of Bulfinch's duplex townhouses.

The Simmons Block was built on Water Street, between Congress and Devonshire Streets, and faced the United States Post Office and Sub-Treasury. Four stories in height, it housed the wares of T.A. Simmons, one of numerous purveyors of ready-made clothing in Boston.

This five-story granite building was at the corner of Franklin and Devonshire Streets. Devonshire Street, on the right, leads toward the Old State House on State Street.

In 1870 Milk Street, just east on Washington Street, had the Old South Meeting House (on the left) and retail stores, including the Boy's Clothing House (far right).

42

Water Street, so named because it was then literally on the harbor's edge, had the Simmons Block on the right and the future site of the United States Post Office and Sub-Treasury on the left. In the distance can be seen Washington Street.

The office of *The Boston Transcript*, a leading newspaper in nineteenth-century Boston, was located at the corner of Washington and Franklin Streets.

Washington Street, looking south of Milk Street, had commercial concerns in this photograph of 1858. Though some of these buildings were converted from onetime residences, the majority were built as shops with warehouse and office space above.

School Street, looking toward Tremont Street from Washington Street, had numerous stores on either side in this photograph of 1858. On the far right is the former Crease House which later became the Old Corner Bookstore in the mid-nineteenth century. Recently, the store closed after many decades as one of Boston's oldest bookstores.

On the right is the old Parker House, at the corner of Tremont and School Streets. Founded by Harvey Parker, the hotel is not only the oldest continuously occupied hotel in the United States, but is also where the Parker House roll and Boston cream pie originated. The granite temple, to the left of the Parker House, was the second headquarters of the Massachusetts Horticultural Society.

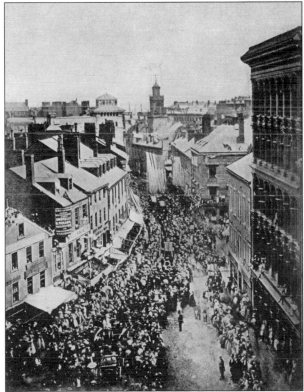

The density of downtown Boston is evident in this c. 1865 photograph of a parade on Court Street. Small buildings sharing a uniform height curve along Court Street on the left, and a high-rise building on the right punctuates the uniformity of the street. In the distance, at the corner of Washington and State Streets, is the Old State House.

The Masonic Temple was a granite Gothic building that was designed by Isaiah Rogers and built in 1830 at the corner of Tremont Street and Temple Place; it served as a Masonic meetingplace until it was sold to the United States government in 1858 for use as a courthouse. A horse-drawn streetcar approaches from Temple Place on the right. On the far left can be seen the columned facade of Saint Paul's Episcopal Church, built in 1819 by Alexander Parris (1780–1852).

Boston City Hall was built in 1863 on School Street by Arthur Gilman and J. Gridley Fox Bryant on the site of Bulfinch's Suffolk County Court House. An impressive example of the French Second Empire style, it replaced the old Bulfinch-designed courthouse and city hall.

The laying of the cornerstone of the United States Post Office and Sub-Treasury attracted thousands of spectators in 1871. Designed by Gridley J. Fox Bryant, the new post office and sub-treasury building was at the junction of Water, Milk and Devonshire Streets and was built of fireproof marble. A hoist lowers the cornerstone on the left, and the spire of the Old South Meeting House can be seen in the distance.

By the time of the Civil War, Boston's population hovered at 165,000 and the former residential aspect of Summer, Franklin, High, and Pearls Streets had given way to commercial concerns. In this photograph of the area, taken from a hot-air balloon, the spire of the Old South Meeting House can be seen on the lower left, which in a diagonal line (representing Washington Street), one can see the crenelated tower of Trinity Church on Summer Street. The streets were lined with closely built granite and stone buildings in a once residential district.

47

A "New Map of Boston Comprising the whole City" was engraved in 1859 for the *Boston Almanac*. The original 800-acre peninsula of Boston had been augmented by the infilling of the new South End (lower left), the Back Bay (upper left), and through the annexation in 1804 of Dorchester Neck (on the right), which was renamed South Boston. The density of the North and South Ends was a compelling reason for the infilling of the marshland surrounding Boston's west coast for new development.

Three

The Great Boston Fire

"Boston In Flames" was a lithograph by Currier and Ives that showed the city afire. The dome of the Massachusetts State House can be seen in the center with flames rising high into the evening sky. In the foreground are small boats, ferries, and excursion ships filled with spectators who watched as Boston was engulfed in flames.

Tebbetts, Baldwin & Davis, wholesale dry goods merchants, was located at the corner of Summer and Kingston Streets, and was where the fire began. A four-story granite building owned by Leman Klous, it had a then fashionable mansard roof (built of wood and sheathed in slate) that allowed for additional storage space. Sharing the building were Damon, Temple and Company, dealers in gloves, lace, and hosiery, and Alexander K. Young and Company, manufacturers of ladies' hoop skirts. At the corner is Signal Box 52, which was from where the first fire call was made on that fateful Saturday night.

Chief Engineer John Stanhope Damrell was Boston's fire chief in 1872. An astute and well-respected manager, he had repeatedly warned the city aldermen of the danger of Boston's unprecedented growth and lack of zoning. His suggestions that water mains and hydrants be replaced for the commercial area, as the extant ones were sufficient only for the once residential area, fell on deaf ears.

The fire spread rapidly into Devonshire Street from Winthrop Square. Hundreds of people swarmed into the center of Winthrop Square carrying trunks filled with business records and whatever else could be salvaged from the burning buildings. Steam fire engines, which firemen dragged by hand due to an epizootic, belch dark smoke as the firemen make a valiant attempt to quell the raging fire, all the while whole buildings were bursting into flames.

Captain Lewis P. Webber was the chief of Engine Company Fourteen on Centre Street in Roxbury, Massachusetts. Two of his horses, unaffected by the epizootic, hauled two fire engines to the scene of the fire and "never did horseflesh find more to do than that upon its arrival at the fire." Webber's wife had given birth to a son on the evening of the fire, and the child was not welcomed by his father until two days later.

The Boston Pilot building was a raging inferno that consumed the entire building within a short time after it caught fire. The mansard roof, constructed of wood supports and sheathed in slate and copper, acted as a vacuum for the flames, which burst through the top of the building at lightning speed. Firemen train their water hoses at the building, but the intensity of the fire was too great for their efforts to be of any real advantage.

Patrick Donahue was the owner of the *Boston Pilot*. Founded in 1836, the *Boston Pilot* was the voice of the Catholic community in Boston. Donahue made a great success of the newspaper and built an impressive building on Franklin Street to house the offices and printing rooms of the paper. The fire caused a loss to Donahue of $300,000. Undaunted, he continued the *Pilot* and in 1878 founded the then popular *Donahue's Monthly Magazine*.

Franklin Street, only completed thirteen years before as a commercial section, caught fire as the flames spread from Summer Street through Arch Street. A large group of spectators crowd the street in the foreground, looking from Washington Street.

Winthrop Square, dominated by the impressive Beebe Block, was in flames within a short period of time, illuminating the night like a torch. Colonel Russell Conwell, in his book *History of the Great Fire in Boston*, said that spectators might "look aghast, and begin to forget the 'Bostonians' stolid faith,' when slate, granite, marble, brick, iron, and steel seemed to flash up as tinder, and glow like furnace-coal."

Looking down Washington Street from Winter Street, firemen have cordoned off spectators as the fire ravages the buildings on the east side of Washington Street. In the center of the etching is the facade of Macullar, Williams and Parker Company, which surprisingly survived the fire. In the distance, at the corner of Milk Street, rises the spire of the Old South Meeting House.

Devonshire Street was aflame by midnight, with the mansard roofs of the commercial blocks raging in flames. It was said that the "great heat created strong currents of air, and caused the winds to whistle about the corners and alleys as fierce and cold as January." Water streams from firehoses could not compete with the intensity of the fire.

Washington Street, looking south from Milk Street, presented a chaotic scene in this etching. On the left is the office of the *Boston Transcript*. The newspaper had recently moved into a new building at the corner of Washington and Franklin Streets.

By Sunday evening, the fire had been stopped, but the ruins on Washington Street would smolder and smoke for days. The facade of Macullar, Williams and Parker Company rises from a rubble-strewn block, and the crenelated tower of Trinity Church on Summer Street can be seen on the left, just past the ruins in the foreground.

Harper's Weekly ("A Journal of Civilization") had an etching of Boston firemen fighting the fire that appeared on their cover (Volume XVI, No. 831) on Saturday, November 30, 1872. The caption read, "Into the Jaws of Death." These firemen fought a valiant battle to contain the fire, especially as they had to pull the fire engines due to an epizootic that disabled nearly all the horses in the city.

Frank Leslie depicted in this print the valiant and successful efforts to save the Old South Meeting House on Washington Street. Threatened with destruction by the rapidly spreading fire, volunteers covered the wood shingle roof with wet blankets as fire engines sprayed water on the spire of the meetinghouse. The Kearsage No. 3 from Portsmouth, New Hampshire, played an integral part in saving this relic of Boston's past.

Looking from the depot of the Hartford and Erie Depot, one sees the ruins of the Great Boston Fire rise like sentinels standing guard over a debris field. The spire of the Old South Meeting House is visible on the left, while the remains of the facade of Saint Stephen's Church on Purchase Street appear eerily on the right.

Looking from Fort Hill, now the area of High Street, the scene of the burnt district was devastating. In the distance, the flames continued to destroy everything in its path. Colonel Conwell, in his eloquent book, said, "Yet the fire paused not, but ran riot with demoniacal glee, as it scorched through the windows, and drove the excited owners away from their own doors."

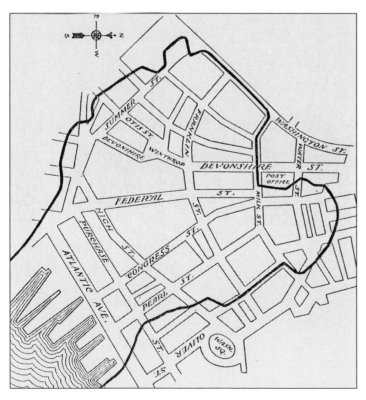

The burnt district was a 40-acre area of what is now Boston's business district. Destroying almost eight hundred buildings, the fire raged through the area bound by Summer, Washington, and Milk Streets, and the waterfront. The area, once residential, had become the pride of Boston with its commercial blocks that were built of granite and marble on the former estates. Almost every structure had the then fashionable mansard roof, which were considered "combustible roofs, like the grass of the prairie, fed the fire as it flew."

Four

The Aftermath:
The Smoke Clears

Steamer No. 10, known as "The Cataract" (from the firehouse on Mount Vernon Street near Charles Street), is on the right with a fireman using a hose to spray the ruins with water. The appearance of the burnt section "was a vast city of ruins, the limit of which could at no point be seen, still smoking and steaming violently from the shock that had caused its fearful overthrow." A group of men stand near the debris on Devonshire Street in front of the new United States Post Office and Sub-Treasury, which can be seen in the distance.

In this view looking down Summer Street from Washington Street, the center of the street has been cleared of debris. On the right are the ruins of Shreve, Crump & Low which were destroyed by a gas explosion the day after the fire was stopped. The crenelated tower of Trinity Church is on the left, and a hook and ladder engine is in the foreground.

Summer Street was a desolate area that had little resemblance to its former appearance other than the cleared streets. Walls and chimneys rise from the ruins showing the extent of the destruction.

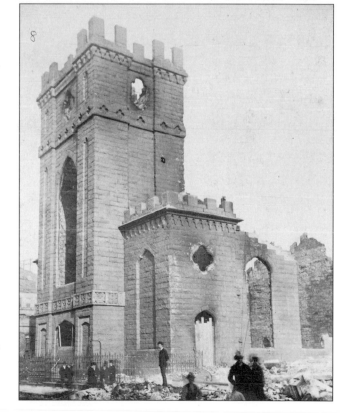

The spire of Trinity Church survived the fire, but the side walls were destroyed. A fireman stands in the right foreground as men converse in front of the church. Reverend Phillips Brooks conducted services on successive Sundays in the hall of the Massachusetts Institute of Technology on Boylston Street in the Back Bay.

The crenelated tower of Trinity Church rises from the rubble-strewn Summer Street on the morning after the fire was stopped. A group of men stand in front of what is now the corner of Summer and Washington Streets, and on the right are the ruins of the Mercantile Buildings at the corner of Summer and Hawley Streets. The studio of William Morris Hunt was also destroyed in the fire, along with his paintings and the numerous European masters displayed in his studio. (Courtesy of David Rooney.)

Looking up Summer Street toward Washington Street, wood staging covers the sidewalk to protect pedestrians from the possibility of falling debris. The crenelated tower of Trinity Church withstood the fire; however, the remainder of the church had to be leveled.

Looking from Washington Street toward Trinity Church, the former site of Weeks and Potter's Company had been reduced to a brick-strewn lot.

The crypt of Trinity Church was laid open by the fire when the interior of the church was destroyed. The west stone wall, punctuated by lancet window openings, rises on the left.

Looking down a passage in the crypt of Trinity Church, one can see that the family vaults have been opened, and the remains of former parishioners were being removed for reburial in such places as Mount Auburn, Mount Hope, Cedar Grove, and Forest Hills Cemeteries. Notice the wood-plank coffins on the left awaiting removal.

From a view looking up Summer Street toward Washington Street, the tower of Trinity Church is visible on the right, and the stores of C.F. Hovey & Company, R.H. Stearns, and Shreve, Crump and Low are on the left. The building of Shreve, Crump and Low was destroyed by an explosion caused by gas seeping from a broken gas pipe the day after the fire. Winter Street, leading to Tremont Street, is in the distance.

The facade of Macullar, Williams and Parker Company survived the fire, but had to be braced by wood planks to stabilize it. Washington Street was the boundary of the fire, and the tower of Trinity Church can be seen on the left.

Looking down Washington Street from Summer Street, one sees the devastation by the fire that had only affected the east side of the street. The spire of the Old South Meeting House is visible in the distance, and the unaffected stores on the west side of Washington Street are on the left.

A member of the Claflin Guards stands on Washington Street in front of the remains of the facade of Macullar, Williams and Parker Company. This poignant photograph shows an elegant marble facade that withstood the fire, but acts as a frame to the devastation that can be seen in the distance. A sign, just behind the guard, informs those interested that the store had moved to the fifth floor at 15 Tremont Street.

Members of the Claflin Guards line up in formation in Liberty Square on November 12, 1872. The guard was called out by the governor to assist the police in maintaining order and to stop looting.

Members of the Claflin Guards stand at attention on the edge of the ruins on Pearl Street. The grotesque remains of the once fashionable granite and brownstone buildings rise like fingers pointing to the sky from the rubble-strewn area.

The spire of the Old South Meeting House, at the corner of Washington and Milk Streets, had been saved by the valiant efforts of firemen and volunteers who protected the roof and spire with wet blankets and a steady stream of water from the Kearsage Engine of Portsmouth, New Hampshire. On the right is the shell of Fowle, Torrey & Company, onetime purveyors of fine carpets. Pieces of granite litter Washington Street, and on the left, signs and awnings of stores unaffected by the fire carry one's eye down the street. (Courtesy of David Rooney.)

Another view of Washington Street, looking north from Franklin Street, shows more of the debris covering the street.

In this view looking down Milk Street from Washington Street, an eerie shadow is cast on the Old South Meeting House from the ruins on the right. In the distance can be seen the area of Post Office Square, with debris littering either side of Milk Street.

The first buildings destroyed by the fire are visible in the center left on Kingston Street, looking from Summer Street.

A fireman speaks with businessmen on Summer Street after the fire. Notice the water hoses in the right foreground.

Purchase Street, seen from Summer Street, had been cleared of debris within a week of the fire, but the devastation was massive, and few walls survived the intensity of the fire.

A man walks past a building at the junction of High and Summer Streets that was one of the few to remain standing, though thoroughly gutted by the fire.

A group of men stand in front of the building at the junction of High and Summer Streets that had survived the fire. On the left are mounds of granite and other debris that had been cleared from Summer Street.

The side walls of a building at the corner of Summer and Broad Streets rise precariously from a brick-strewn street. A sign on the right proclaims that *Boston In Flames*, a booklet on the fire, was ready and available for purchase.

From this angle looking north from Summer Street, one can see that the fire had levelled most of the downtown district. Columns have fallen on top of the granite and bricks that were once part of elegant commercial blocks. In the distance can be seen the tower of Trinity Church and the Park Street Church.

Standing on Milk Street, a group of men gaze at the ruins of the buildings in and around Liberty Square, near the Mason Building, where the fire was eventually stopped. (Courtesy of David Rooney.)

Franklin Street was a scene of devastation following the fire. Within a week, small tents and wood shacks were erected as the streets were cleared of debris for ease of passage. The spire of the Park Street Church rises on the left and that of the Old South Meeting House on the right.

On Franklin Street, a group of businessmen sit and stand in the midst of the ruins of the once elegant buildings that had lined the street. In the distance is the partially completed United States Post Office and Sub-Treasury building, with its roof staging on the far left.

Looking down Franklin Street from Washington Street, this view shows that the street was almost completely obliterated by the fire.

A man gazes at the ruins of a building on Franklin Street. Bricks seem to be everywhere, spewing forth from the site into the street.

Standing on a partially cleared sidewalk on Franklin Street, a man looks from four projecting ruins of the once elegant commercial buildings. Notice the quoining of the ruin on the left.

Men stand near a sign at 96 Devonshire Street which alerts those interested that the company formerly here, George C. Richardson and Company, had moved to the corner of Chauncey and Bedford Streets. (Courtesy of the Boston Athenaeum.)

Franklin Street, prior to its clearing, was a virtual sea of granite pieces that had fallen when the buildings were destroyed by the fire.

Two men stand by the one of the open vaults of the Bank of North America on Devonshire Street.

A group of merchants and their employees pose for their photograph among the ruins of their former places of business. The granite seemed to melt with the intensity of the heat, and the ruins on the right have a grotesque look to them.

Standing on either side of huge mounds of clothing are merchants and workmen in the Post Office Square area. The clothing had been part of the stock of Freeland, Harding and Richardson's store on Devonshire Street; on the left is the partially completed post office, which withstood the fire due to the use of fireproof materials in its construction. (Courtesy of The Boston Athenaeum.)

Steamer No. 10, known as "The Cataract," was placed on Devonshire Street in Post Office Square to allow firemen to hose down the smoldering ruins and to stop any small fires that might have flared up. A group of men stand in front of the ruins of buildings on Milk Street. The new post office can be seen in the distance. (Courtesy of The Boston Athenaeum.)

Workmen pause in their clean-up efforts to pose for one of the omnipresent photographers who descended upon the burnt district after the fire. A canvas tent and a small wood shed have been erected in what is now Post Office Square, and on the right is the Old South Meeting House on Milk Street.

Looking northeast from Franklin Street, the ruins of the fire could be compared to a sea of debris. On the left center can be seen the unfinished United States Post Office and Sub-Treasury building.

Looking toward the new Post Office and Sub-Treasury, one sees the walls of buildings destroyed by the fire, and the surrounding piles of bricks.

The facade of the new Post Office and Sub-Treasury seemed oddly out of place considering the extent of the ruins. Federal Street was cleared of debris within a week of the fire, allowing access to the area by merchants and city crews.

The temporary post office for Boston was opened in Fanueil Hall in the Dock Square area for those affected by the fire, before being moved to the Old South Meeting House. In this print of the time, men ascend the staircase to obtain mail, while guards stand at attention.

The panorama, from the new Post Office and Sub-Treasury, of the fire's destruction was almost mind-boggling in the extent of the devastation.

From a view looking south from the new Post Office and Sub-Treasury, it was as if entire buildings had been swept away by the fire, leaving just bricks and chunks of granite to mark their former location.

A panoramic view of the devastation wrought by the great fire, as seen from Purchase Street looking toward Summer and Washington Streets, was captured about a week after the fire was stopped. Woodsheds have been erected in the foreground, and most of the streets have been cleared of debris for ease of transportation. The dome of the Massachusetts State House can be seen on the right, flanked by the spires of the Park Street Church (on the left) and the Old South Meeting House.

Kilby Street, looking toward State Street, had a macabre aspect with the facades of buildings completely gone and their exposed, gutted shells. A fireman is flanked by men in front of 52 Kilby Street, the site of the Andrew C. Spring and Company. (Courtesy of The Boston Athenaeum.)

The ruins of the Bank of North America on Devonshire Street included a vertical pier of granite that rose from a bed of bricks.

Lincoln Street, near the corner of Summer Street, had entire blocks destroyed, but many of the facades remained standing.

At the corner of Water and Congress Streets, looking southeast, the ruins of these buildings appear to be like thin wafers projecting from the debris.

Congress Street, looking toward State Street, had been cleared of rubble, but the bricks, granite chunks, and all matter of debris were piled high on either side of the street, waiting to be cleared.

A wall of bricks rises from the ruins of buildings along Congress Street.

Looking toward Congress Street from Water Street, this photograph shows men standing before the remains of commercial buildings.

The Old South Meeting House was saved by the valiant efforts of firemen and volunteers who threw wet blankets on the roof and sprayed water on the spire. The meetinghouse's spire stands unharmed by the fire among a rubble-strewn Milk Street.

The Old South Block on Milk Street, just across the street from the Old South Meeting House, had oddly shaped ruins that included a portion of the first floor of the building on the right and the ruins of brick walls on the left.

Pearl Street was entirely destroyed by the fire, yet the facades of these buildings survived to shield interiors that were completely obliterated. Here, from the left, are 59, 55, and 53 Pearl Street, or what remained of them.

Another view of Pearl Street shows how most buildings were levelled by the intensity of the fire, but also that an entire block's facade might remarkably survive to give the effect of an ancient aqueduct-type appearance to the ruins.

A group of men pose outside the ruins of a building on Pearl Street.

A group of men on Pearl Street discuss the fire.

At the corner of High and Pearl Streets is a group of men with the projecting ruins in the background.

In this photograph, a man stands guard over a safe outside 25 Pearl Street. Many of the safes were recovered in the weeks following the fire, with some of the contents intact; however, for the most part safes fell through the floors to the cellars where they baked in the heat of the smoldering coals in furnace rooms.

With relocation signs projecting from the debris like headstones in a cemetery, these men flank a pile of bricks that seemingly continues for blocks, with few variations.

The ruins of Shreve, Crump and Low on Summer Street near Washington Street were not the result of the fire but a gas explosion. On Sunday night, November 10, 1872, a second fire erupted as the underground gas pipes on Summer Street exploded, causing further destruction in the area now referred to as the "Burnt Out District." (Courtesy of David Rooney.)

"Columbia Lays Aside Her Laurels to Mourn at the Burning of Her Birthplace," was the caption of this sketch by Thomas Nast. The serpent-coiffed devil can be seen sweeping above with fire in tow as "Columbia" casts aside her laurel wreaths earned for National Victory on November 5, 1872, and Foreign Arbitration in regards to San Juan and the Alabama Claims.

The remaining portion of this granite facade looked like melted sugar candy after the effects of the fire. The intensity of the heat of the fire caused a large amount of the granite to literally melt, creating stark and grotesque shapes that projected from the ruins.

Relics of the Great Boston Fire included metal plates, cups and saucers, and assorted pieces of tableware that were soldered together by the heat of the fire. Sold as curiosities at the time, it seemed inevitable that every local historical society in the Boston area would eventually receive some "relic" of the fire's devastation.

"Homeless Tonight, or Boston In Ashes" was the cover to sheet music that was composed in commemoration of the Great Boston Fire of 1872. (Courtesy of the Boston Athenaeum.)

Five

A Phoenix Arises

After the fire, Summer Street was rebuilt with impressive buildings five and six stories in height. On the left is the former site of Church Green, the junction of Bedford and Summer Streets; the street on the right is Devonshire Street. In the distance is the spire of the Park Street Church. Horse-drawn delivery wagons line both sides of the thriving commercial district once known as the "Burnt District." (Courtesy of William Dillon.)

The site where the fire began, at the corner of Summer and Kingston Streets, was rebuilt with a four-story granite building with a modified mansard roof that still survives today.

In the years immediately after the fire, Summer Street became a major street, with offices and warehouses being built on the site of the mansions designed by Bulfinch. In the distance is the spire of the Park Street Church. (Courtesy of William Dillon.)

George A. Clough was elected ten times the architect of the city of Boston, and he oversaw many of the new buildings being built after the Great Boston Fire of 1872. The first architect to be elected city architect (in 1874), he was to shape the image of Boston with well-designed buildings, much like Charles Bulfinch had done nearly a century before.

By the turn of the century, the corner of Summer and Devonshire Streets was built with the banking house of the Commonwealth Trust Company, which had replaced the six-story building of the Manufacturers National Bank.

Smith Patterson Company, a business of diamond merchants, jewelers, and silversmiths, was located at 52 Summer Street at the corner of Hawley Street. A five-story building that was completed in 1876, it later became Kennedy's Department Store and today has been preserved as part of a high-rise office tower.

The Rice and Hutchins Buildings were built between 2 and 20 High Street on the corner of Summer Street. A notable shoe manufacturer, especially of the "Educator Shoes," this company constructed their building on the former site of Daniel Webster's house and garden.

The Manufacturers National Bank was an impressive six-story building at the corner of Summer and Devonshire Streets. Notice the clock set prominently on the sixth floor of the facade.

The first floor interior of the Manufacturers National Bank had the tellers' cages near the entrance and the clerks' desks on the far right.

Franklin Street, looking east from Washington Street, was rebuilt following the fire with impressive buildings that followed the graceful curve of Bulfinch's Tontine Crescent. The Mechanics National Bank, with an impressive four-sided street clock, dominated the corner now occupied by Woolworth's. A streetcar stops to allow passengers to enter the car in the center of Franklin Street, c. 1885. (Courtesy of William Dillon.)

The National Revere Bank was a Ruskinian Gothic building at 100 Franklin Street. Incorporated in 1859, the bank was one of the numerous banking houses to promptly rebuild after the fire.

The National Bank of North America was at 106 Franklin Street. Organized in 1850 as a state bank, it was nationalized in 1864. The bank shared the space with N. Boynton & Company and Jones, McDuffie & Stratton.

The Forbes Lithograph-Manufacturing Company was located in this fabulous Ruskinian Gothic Revival building at the corner of Franklin and Devonshire Streets. On the left side of the building is the National Revere Bank, which faces on Franklin Street.

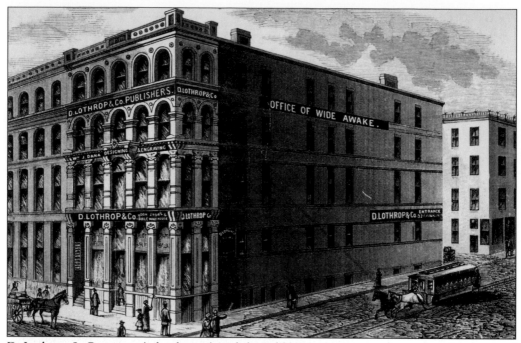

D. Lothrop & Company (a bookstore) and the Bible Warehouse were located at the corner of Franklin and Hawley Streets. As the sign proudly proclaims, the building was also the office of *Wide Awake*, a popular periodical in the late nineteenth century.

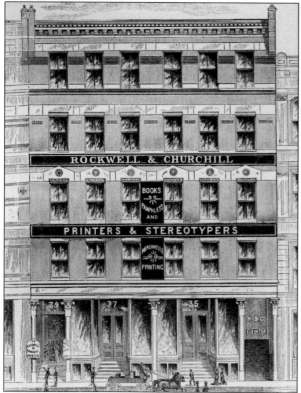

Rockwell & Churchill's Printing House was at 35 and 37 Arch Street.

Lee & Shepard, publishers, was located at the corner of Franklin and Hawley Streets and was in the last quarter of the nineteenth century the "largest book-publishers, importers and dealers in New England."

The first floor of Lee & Shepard was a popular place to peruse new books, or as we see on the far right, to sit down and read in comfort.

Washington Street, looking north from Summer Street on the right, became a bustling shopping district after the Great Fire of 1872. The buildings on the left of the street were not affected by the fire and remained to face the "New Boston" being built on the right. Horse-drawn streetcars traversed this busy area, connecting the Back Bay, South End, and South Boston areas of the city.

Jordan, Marsh & Company, designed by the architectural firm of Winslow & Wetherall, was considered the largest department store in New England in the late nineteenth century, and their store occupied the entire block of Summer, Washington, Avon, and Chauncey Streets. With "66 departments, 3,500 employees and 15 acres of floor space," it was the pride and joy of Eben D. Jordan, founder of the store in 1841.

The Macullar Parker Company's facade on Washington Street, on the right, survived the fire, and the company rebuilt their shop within a short period of time. As a manufacturer of clothing for men and boys, they had been providing ready-made clothing since 1849.

One of the workshops of the Macullar Parker Company had dozens of seamstresses working at long worktables on both mens' and boys' clothing.

The third floor of the Macullar Parker Company was the Boys' Clothing Workshop, where fabric was cut by tailors to a specific pattern and the initial sewing was done by the seamstresses (on the left).

The *Boston Transcript*, a leading daily newspaper, rebuilt their newspaper building on the same site it occupied at the time of the fire, the corner of Washington and Franklin Streets. Founded in 1830, the newspaper was an independent Republican newspaper owned by the heirs of Henry W. Dutton.

The Old South Church, which survived the fire through the valiant efforts of the firemen and of Kearsage 3, was remodeled for use by the United State Post Office following the fire. On either side of the spire, two-story brick additions were built and used until the new post office was completed.

After the post office left the Old South Meeting House, it was thought that the church would be demolished to make way for a new building because its congregation had recently moved to a new edifice in the Back Bay. Bostonians' reactions were swift and vociferous, and through the leadership of Mary Porter Tileston Hemenway, a great philanthropist, the building was saved not just as a historic site, but as an important educational center for the history of Boston.

Built in 1729, the Old South Meeting House is the oldest place of worship in downtown Boston. Thanks to the persistent efforts of Mary Hemenway, the Old South Meeting House Association was formed and today operates the former meetinghouse as a major attraction on Boston's Freedom Trail.

Washington Street, seen from Winter Street, had a bustling quality by the late 1880s with streetcars passing along the center of the street as shoppers crowd the sidewalks during business hours. The spire of the Old South Meeting House can be seen in the distance.

Washington Street, looking north from Franklin Street, had numerous shops and businesses that made going to "Town" for shopping a special occasion.

Washington Street had prominent stores, such as Wood & Dodge, Raymond's, and Lewis Brothers, in the new buildings that were constructed between Franklin and Milk Streets.

In a view looking east on Milk Street, as seen from Washington Street, the Old South Meeting House is visible on the left and some of the new buildings on the right.

The buildings on Milk Street that were completed by 1875 were draped with bunting in honor of the centennial of the Battle of Bunker Hill on June 17, 1875. The Centennial Lunch Room can be seen on the far left, and the next two buildings were built on the site of Benjamin Franklin's birthplace. (Courtesy of The Boston Athenaeum.)

The rebuilt area of downtown Boston, such as Milk Street seen here, had modern and architecturally significant buildings that created an urbane commercial district. A horse-drawn wagon carries a load of beer barrels and turns into Post Office Square, c. 1890.

Milk Street, looking east from Arch Street, was rebuilt with superb buildings, such as the Equitable Building designed between 1873 and 1875 by Arthur Gilman (second from right) and the double building of the New York Mutual Life Insurance Company and the New England Mutual Life Insurance Company. The bunting, decorating many of the buildings, was in honor the centennial of the Battle of Bunker Hill in 1875. (Courtesy of the BPL.)

The American Bell Telephone Company's building was constructed at 125 Milk Street, facing Post Office Square as an impressive eight-story building with monumental Romanesque arches. The telephone was to become an important part of the development of Boston after its invention in 1877 by Alexander Graham Bell.

The Operating Room and Switchboard of the New England Telephone and Telegraph Company was a busy place with operators seated before individual, fifty-wire switchboards.

The United States Post Office and Sub-Treasury was not severely damaged by the Great Boston Fire of 1872, and the marble used in its construction was unharmed by the flames. Designed by A.B. Mullet and completed in 1873, the building faced Post Office Square and was bound by Milk Street on the left and Water Street on the right; the square was the area between Water, Milk, Congress, and Pearl Streets and was named in 1874. Today, the John W. McCormack Post Office and Court House building stands on this site.

The New York Life Insurance Company, on the left, was built in 1874–1875 by Peabody and Stearns, while the New England Mutual Life Insurance Company was built in 1873 by noted architect Nathaniel J. Bradlee (1829–1888) on Milk Street, facing Post Office Square. A streetcar travels along Congress Street on the right.

Though not identical, the two buildings of the New York and the New England Mutual Life Insurance Companies shared similar details. However, a clock tower punctuates the mansard roof on the left and a group statue caps the mansard roof on the right.

Nathaniel J. Bradlee designed the New England Mutual Life Insurance Company to gracefully follow the curve of Congress Street. The two-storied mansard roof had projecting dormers and chimneys that seemed to march along the roof, carrying one's eye along the structure.

The United States Post Office and Sub-Treasury dominated Post Office Square with its impressive central building being capped by a large mansard roof and flanked by symmetrical wings. Two enormous sculptural ensembles by Daniel Chester French, *Commerce* and *Industry*, flanked the central pavilion. In the foreground is a monument to George Thorndike Angell (1823–1909), founder of the Massachusetts Society of Prevention of Cruelty to Animals.

Congress Street, looking from Post Office Square, was rebuilt following the fire with impressive buildings of diverse architectural styles. (Courtesy of William Dillon.)

The United States Custom House was built in 1847 by Ammi Burnham Young, at the original harbor's edge. An impressive Doric-columned granite building, the dome was replaced in 1915 by an 495-foot, thirty-story office tower designed by Peabody and Stearns. Today, the Custom House has been restored by Marriott Corporation, and is an elegant time-sharing residence as the Marriott Vacation Club International.

The Boston Chamber of Commerce, later known as the Grain Exchange, was erected between 1890 and 1892 at the junction of India Street and Central Wharf. Designed by Shepley, Rutan and Coolidge, successors to H.H. Richardson, it is a rough-hewn pink Worcester granite Romanesque Revival building with a series of peaked dormers surrounding the tower's conical roof.

The Trade Room of the Boston Chamber of Commerce was a circular room with a large chandelier suspended from a domed ceiling that was 38 feet above the floor. The Boston Chamber of Commerce was described in 1915 as one of the "most aggressive commercial bodies in any American city."

Looking up State Street from the corner of Broad Street, the Old State House can be seen in the distance at the head of the avenue. State Street was once the financial quarter of the city and had numerous banks and investment houses.

Originally known as King Street prior to the Revolution, it was renamed State Street in 1784. On both sides of the street in this photograph are buildings representing architectural styles from the entire spectrum of the nineteenth century, from small brick buildings on the left to the high-rise structures of the late nineteenth century.

H.A. Johnson & Company was located at 222 and 224 State Street, where the company was the manufacturer of "bakers and confectioners' supplies, jams, jellies, preserves and pie filene [filling]."

The corner of Franklin and Devonshire Streets, looking north toward State Street, had large office buildings flanking each corner. On the left is the Boston Safe Deposit and Trust Company.

State Street, seen from the balcony of the Old State House, was a sea of flags on Flag Day in 1915.

The Exchange Building, an Italian Renaissance office building, was built in 1891 on State Street, between Kilby and Congress Streets, and was designed by Peabody and Stearns. This was the home of the Boston Stock Exchange for many years, and is today part of Exchange Place. ❧

The interior of the Boston Stock Exchange was an impressive domed room with trading stations placed strategically throughout on the floor for stockbrokers.

The head of State Street had the Old State House as its major focus. Built in 1711, it was saved by the Bostonian Society in 1882 from ignominious obscurity after decades of commercial use. Restored, it is today a major attraction on Boston's Freedom Trail. On the right is the New England Merchants' Bank; the city's first skyscraper, the Ames Building, designed in 1888 by Shepley, Rutan and Coolidge and named for Governor Ames, rises in the rear. (Courtesy of William Dillon.)

Looking down Washington Street, the Rogers, Sears (designed by Cummings and Sears), and Ames Buildings can be seen on the left with Scollay Square in the distance.

Scollay Square, named for Boston merchant John Scollay, was the junction of Washington, Court, and State Streets and was considered one of Boston's liveliest spots at the turn of the century. Streetcars of the Metropolitan Railroad travel along the street and connect all parts of the city and the suburbs, as people go about their business in carriages, carts, wagons, and by foot. (Courtesy of William Dillon.)

Scollay Square, looking west from Washington Street, was a bustling retail and entertainment district at the turn of the century. A statue of John Winthrop is in the center foreground; the stores on the left were replaced in the 1960s with Boston City Hall Plaza, and on the right is the famous Crawford House, where Sally Keith reigned by the flick of her tassels. (Courtesy of William Dillon.)

Tremont Street, looking north from West Street, was unaffected by the Great Boston Fire; however, it was a major route for streetcars connecting all parts of the city in the months following the fire. The spire of Peter Banner's Park Street Church of 1809 can be seen just beyond the Boston Common on the left.

South Street was entirely rebuilt between 1873 and 1876 with five-story commercial buildings on both sides of the street.

The building of Fenno Brothers & Childs at 117 Federal Street was typical of the structures built after the fire in Boston's commercial district. Fenno Brothers & Child were wool commission merchants, and their business shared this Gothic style building with the H.W. Johns Manufacturing Company.

Mills, Knight & Company was located at 60 Pearl Street at the corner of Wendell Street. Built of brownstone, this impressive building extended from 60 to 78 Pearl Street and replaced buildings destroyed by the fire.

Batchelder & Lincoln Company was located at 94, 96, and 98 Federal Street where they were "wholesale dealers in boots, shoes and rubbers, shoe store supplies, leather, and findings." Founded in 1852, the company promptly rebuilt after the fire and within a decade had one hundred and fifty employees and eighteen traveling salesmen.

Acknowledgments

I would like to thank the following for their assistance in the researching and writing of this photographic book on the Great Boston Fire of 1872. In many instances, these individuals have loaned photographs, stereoviews, and books on the fire and its aftermath. I deeply appreciate their continued support and interest:

Daniel J. Ahlin, Anthony Bognanno, The Boston Athenaeum, Sally Robbins Bradshaw, Paul and Helen Graham Buchanan, Mary Jo Campbell, Jamie Carter, Elise Ciregna, Elizabeth Williams Clapp, Margaret Harriman Clarke, Lorna Condon (Society for the Preservation of New England Antiquities), Mary G. Connell, Emily Curran (the Old South Meetinghouse Association), Rupert A.M. Davis, Dexter, William Dillon, Catherine Eisenmann, Paul R. Finn, Martha Buchanan Forte, Edward W. Gordon (president of the Victorian Society, New England Chapter), Jack Grinold, Helen Hannon, Pauline Chase Harrell, Barbara Adams Hebard, Mabel Marie Herweg, Stephen Hill, Ann Marie Gionet Hubing, Kevin Huffman, Kiki Kneeland, Sally Ann Kydd, James Z. Kyprianos, Robert J. MacMillan (M.D.), Ellen Washburn Martin, The Old South Meetinghouse Association, Anne Marie Moore, Bob Murphy, Stephen and Susan Paine, William H. Pear, Mary Melvin Petronella, Jeannette Lithgow Peverly, Sally Pierce (The Print Room of The Boston Athenaeum), Brian Powell, Roger Prouty, Barbara M. Pugliese, David Rooney, Joseph Russo, Dennis Ryan, Anthony and Mary Mitchell Sammarco, the late Charlotte Tuttle Clapp Sammarco, Rosemary Sammarco, Robert Bayard Severy, Catherina Slautterback (The Print Room of The Boston Athenaeum), Verity Carslile Smith, Joyce Stevens of Heritage Education, Anne and George Thompson, Kenneth Turino, William Varrell, Dorothy C. Wallace, The West Roxbury Historical Society, Virginia M. White, Lewis Whitlock, and the members of The Victorian Society, New England Chapter.

A portion of the royalties from the sale of this book will benefit The Victorian Society, New England Chapter, which in 1997 is celebrating the 25th anniversary of the chapter's founding.